MW01244232

99 SUPERIOR AFFIRMATIONS

*"THAT WILL CERTAINLY ALTER
THE COURSE OF YOUR DESTINY"*

Eiman " Sheikhy Chic" Makki
Published By: Your world is Yours
(YWY) LLC

Other Published Works, Books & Materials

1. **"The Advancing Individual"**
*12 Attitudinal Dispositions
That Guarantee Personal Advancement" ($19.99)*

2. **"How To Not Be Poor"**
Mental Cures Against Poverty, Lack & Scarcity ($19.99)

3. **"Believe & Manifest"**
*The Poetically Systematic Science
Of Belief, Faith & Manifestation ($19.99)*

4. **"The Best Kept Secret"**
*Your Hidden Eternal Identity & The Most Factual Scientific
Reasonings Which Prove You Were Born Perfect ($19.99)*

Purchase & Acquire Here

Copyright © 2023 By Eiman "Sheikhy Chic" Makki

All Rights Reserved

TABLE OF CONTENTS

Your World is Yours

You Are To Become Everything
You Were Intended To Become.

These Thoughts Are Powerful, Grand, Illustrious, Noble &
Eminent Thoughts, Which Are *Empowering.*

May These Thoughts Accelerate Your Ascension
& Expedite Your Arrival To Your Truth Which Always
Was.

- *Sheikh Eiman Makki*

INTRODUCTION

Your World is Yours

I welcome all people, student, pupils & disciples to this
brief & extremely potent document, which has been
manifested with the intention to affirm, impel & impress
higher principles as well as UNIVERSAL TRUTHS upon
the PSYCHE of its beholder.

•

The age-old adage goes <u>"As a (hu)man thinketh so he/they</u>
<u>will be"</u> so this brief & extremely potent pamphlet is
designed to instill & install
specific high-quality thoughts intended to
CORRECT & OVERWRITE flawed thinking/thoughts
which may be currently be present.

•

The greatest aim of any constructively intellectual mind is
to create as much distance as possible between
<u>oneself & erroneous conclusions.</u>

Therefore, Sheikh Eiman Makki has created & listed a
series of statements which are indeed true for all who exist

& inhabit the boundless
magical universe we all happen to occupy.

•

This list of thoughts & statements can be applied to & by
anyone who is willing to plant the seeds of said thoughts &
statements into their mental garden.
These thoughts are for those ready & willing to begin
becoming the landscapers & architects of their mental
garden & personal mental-infrastructure

•

Your world is Yours is a mindset, a frame of belief & a
mental operating system primed & premised upon mental
identification with objective laws
& dis-identification with the subjective laws of man
i.e., based upon the identification with factual actuality over
subjective realities, so that all who make informed
discernments may align themselves
& their actions with supreme natural laws.

•

By embodying this mindset, we become free from mental
enslavement to ignorance, benightment & falsehood, thus
entering a new personal age of self-experience founded
upon enlightenment
& self-mastery.

•

Following this introduction page will be a series of
affirmations designed to reinforce in & to (INTO) the
subconscious mind of all readers, the absolute truths by

which we will hold ourselves to.
Which are our new elite mental standard.

•

By reaffirming these absolute facts daily for at least 30 days
we will make sure to achieve the highest level of faith by
annihilating & uprooting any seeds which may be lurking as
weeds in our ever-sacred metaphoric proverbial mental
gardens.

If at any point you read an affirmation
& your heart tells you it hasn't been true,
All you must do is carry it forward with you
into the future & it will be true.
"As you believe so it will be done unto you"
"Ratio Deciendi: Principium Triumphi Praecedentis"
— Sheikh M. 10/17/2023

YOUR WORLD IS YOURS, ALWAYS & FOREVER

YOU ARE NOW ABOUT TO EXPIRIENCE

99 AFFIRMATIONS WHICH WILL CERTAINLY
ALTER THE COURSE OF YOUR DESTINY
ايمن شيخ مكي

BEGINNING

Your World is Yours

1

"I CHOOSE TO ONLY PLANT CONSTRUCTIVE THOUGHTS SEEDS *IN THE GARDEN OF MY MIND.*"

2

"I EMBODY DISCIPLINE, I EMBODY PRINCIPLE & JUST-CAUSE OVER CAPRICE & PLEASURE."

3

"I WILL READ OVER THESE AFFIRMATIONS *TWICE A DAY FOR 30 DAYS.*"

4

"WITH THESE AFFIRMATIONS I AM MAKING CONSCIOUS-CONSTRUCTIVE SUGGESTIONS TO MY SUBCONSCIOUS MIND."

5

"I MAY ENCOUNTER
RESISTANCE FROM OLD
WAYS OF THINKING & I
WILL CONFRONT THEM
DIRECTLY & CONQUER
THEM WITH MY ULTIMATE
DESIRE FOR CORRECTED
THINKING & THOUGHTS."

6

"MY WORLD IS MINE
_& I AM ITS RIGHTFUL
MASTER."

7

"MY MIND IS MINE & I SHALL FEED & BUILD IT IN ACCORDANCE WITH UNIVERSAL TRUTH."

8

"*MY BODY IS MINE*

& I SHALL ONLY FEED,

APPLY & MAKE USE OF IT

IN A CONSTRUCTIVE

WAY."

9

"MY SOUL IS MINE FOR ETERNITY I AM WHO I AM & I WILL BE WHO I WILL BE FOR ETERNITY"

10

"I AM BLESSED
& ALIVE
BY MEANS BEYOND
MY PERSONAL WILL
& COMPREHENSION."

11

"I HAVE BEEN WILLED INTO EXISTENCE BY THE MOST SUPREME OF ALL INFLUENCES & POWERS"

12

"THE CREATOR OF ALL CREATION HAS GIVEN ME EVERYTHING I NEED TO SUCCEED."

13

"IT IS UP TO ME TO DO THE NECESSARY WORK TO MANIFEST THE REST."

14

"I DEVOID MYSELF OF ENTITLEMENT & FULLY EMBRACE AN EARNING-MINDSET."

15

"I DESERVE TO EXIST AS LONG AS I AM WILLING TO EARN MY EXISTENCE & SUSTENANCE."

16

"I UNDERSTAND THAT IF ONE DOES NOT, WORK ONE MAY NOT EAT, SO I WILL EARN."

17

"I OPERATE FROM SUPREME SCIENCE NOT BIAS, DOGMA OR SUPERSTITION."

18

"WHATEVER IT IS THAT I DESIRE I WILL ATTRACT, SO I MAKE SURE TO ONLY DESIRE CONSTRUCTIVE THINGS."

19 "I LOVE MYSELF."

20

"I WILL PROTECT MYSELF ESPECIALLY FROM MY DESTRUCTIVE SELF."

21 "I RESPECT MYSELF."

22

**"I AM FULLY CONSCIOUS THAT
I ONLY HAVE ONE LIFE &
WITH THIS ONE LIFE I WILL
MAKE THE ABSOLUTE BEST OF
IT IN HONOR OF THE FACT
THAT I HAVE BEEN WILLED
INTO EXISTENCE
INDEPENDENT OF MY OWN
ACTIONS BY THE MOST
SUPREME POWER IN ALL OF
EXISTENCE."**

23

"I RESONATE
& VIBRATE IN SUPREME
GRATITUDE TOWARD THE
HIGHEST OF POWERS &
ALL OF EXISTENCE."

24

"I WILL ACT IN ACCORDANCE WITH MY HIGHER WILL."

25

"I WILL END ALL NEGOTIATIONS WITH MY LESSER SELF."

26

"I DO NOT SEEK A POSITIVE VIBRATION AS *I AM A POSITIVE VIBRATION.*"

27

"I AM ETERNALLY INEXTRICABLY LINKED TO ALL THAT IS & ALL THAT WILL EVER BE."

28 *"I TRUST MYSELF."*

29

"I IDENTIFY AS AN INDEPENDENT
INDIVIDUATION & EXPRESSION OF
ALL WITHIN ALL & YET STILL
SIMULTANEOUSLY RECOGNIZE I AM
INEXTRICABLE TO THE ALL
THEREFORE
I AM ALL."

30

"THE GREATEST SIN IS PERCEIVED SEPARATENESS."

31

"THE BIGGER PICTURE & GREATER GOOD ARE MORE IMPORTANT THAN MY PERSONAL PERSONA."

32

"I ACCEPT THAT MY RESULTS ARE ABSOLUTELY CONTINGENT UPON THE QUALITY OF MY ACTIONS, I.E., THE QUALITY OF MY CONDUCT."

33

"THE OBJECTIVE UNIVERSE
CONSPIRES IN MY FAVOR
AS LONG AS
I AM IN ACCORDANCE WITH
ITS FAVORS, THAT IS TO SAY
IN FAVOR OF INCREASED
POWER & HARMONY FOR
ALL."

34

"THE NATURAL LAW OF THE UNIVERSE IS ABUNDANCE. POVERTY IS ILLNESS"

35

"I CANNOT LIVE OR BE ANY OTHER WAY AFTER AFFIRMING THESE IRREFUTABLE FACTS."

36

"I POSSESS UNLIMITED MENTAL STRENGTH."

37

"I POSSESS UNLIMITED SPIRITUAL STRENGTH."

38

"I POSSESS AN UNBREAKABLE WILL."

39

"I CHANGE MY THOUGHTS; THEREFORE, I CHANGE MY LIFE."

40

"I KNOW WHERE
I AM GOING."

41

"THE PATH WILL
ILLUMINATE
AS I WALK IT,
THIS IS BECAUSE
I AM THE LIGHT."

42

"I AM UNLIMITED IN POTENTIAL."

43

"I ACTIVELY SEEK TO
IDENTIFY & DETECT ANY
SELF-IMPOSED LIMITS IN
ORDER TO REPLACE THEM
WITH THE UNBRIDLED
BELIEF IN MY OWN
ABILITIES."

44

"THE BEST THINGS IN LIFE ARE ALWAYS ATTRACTED TO ME."

45

"I WILL FEED MYSELF COURAGE IN THE FACE OF ANY DOUBT OR FEARS."

46

"I PROTECT & INNOCULATE MY MIND FROM ALL EXTERNAL IMPRESSIONS NAMLEY DOUBT, FEAR & WORRY."

47

"I WILL ALWAYS ACHIEVE EXACTLY THAT WHICH DESIRE."

48

"I WILL CREATE THE GREATEST DEGREE OF PHYSICAL, SPIRITUAL, MENTAL, EMOTIONAL & EXISTENTIAL SATISFACTION FOR MYSELF."

49

"I HAVE FAITH IN THE
UNSEEN FORCES WHICH
GOVERN ALL OF
EXISTENCE AS WELL AS MY
OWN PERSONAL
SUBCONSCIOUS TO SEE TO
IT THAT I ACHIEVE
EXACTLY THAT WHICH MY
HEART DESIRES."

50

"I AM ALREADY EXTREMELY TALENTED, I MUST MASTERFULLY DEVELOP MY TALENTS."

51

"I AM EXTREMELY SKILLED I MUST MASTERFULLY DEVELOP MY SKILLS."

52

"I VALUE MY MIND, BODY & SPIRIT."

53

"I DO NOT TAKE MY MIND,
BODY & SPIRIT FOR
GRANTED; THEY ARE
TEMPORARY GIFTS FROM
THE DIVINE WHICH I DID
NOT EARN & WHICH CAN &
WILL BE TAKEN AWAY."

54

"IN THIS MOMENT
I HAVE EVOLVED
& WILL SUSTAIN
MY DESIRE TO EVOLVE
FOR ETERNITY."

55

"I BECOME WHAT I THINK ABOUT THEREFORE

I ONLY THINK OF CONSTRUCTIVE THINGS."

56

"HOUSES DO NOT BUILD
THEMSELVES THEREFORE
I MUST REMAIN
CONSTRUCTIVELY DUTIFUL
TOWARD MYSELF, MY LIFE &
MY VISION."

57

"I AM DEDICATED TO PERSONAL EXCELLENCE & PERSONAL DEVELOPMENT."

58 "I HAVE A SET TARGET BEFORE ME."

59

"I HOLD CRYSTAL-CLEAR-VISIONS OF ALL THAT I WOULD LIKE TO ACHIEVE, YES, I DO."

60

"I AM INTELLIGENT."

61

"I POSSESS GREAT INTELLECT."

62

"I AM EXTREMELY
KNOWLEDGEABLE IN & ON
ALL SUBJECTS OF EARTH AS
WELL AS THE WHOLE
BOUNDLESS UNIVERSE."

63

"I AM RESPONSIBLE FOR MY OWN EMOTIONS."

64

"I AM NOT PERSONALLY RESPONSIBLE FOR THE MIS-MANAGED EMOTIONS OF OTHERS."

65

"I KNOW THAT MY INTENT IS PURE."

66

"I KNOW THAT I AM INNOCENT, BECAUSE I MEAN NO HARM."

67

"THERE IS NO ILL WILL IN THE CONSTITUTION OF MY SOUL."

68

**"I LIVE TO SERVE THE
MOST-HIGH & NEVER
ANYTHING WHICH IS
EVEN ONE IOTA
LESSER IN DEGREE."**

69

"I WILL ENLIGHTEN ALL THOSE WHO COME ACROSS MY PATH."

70

"FINANCIAL INDEPENDENCE BELONGS TO ME."

71

"I GET EVERYTHING THAT I EVER WANT IN LIFE."

72

"I AM ONE OF THE CREATOR OF CREATIONS MOST FAVORED CREATIONS."

73

"I HAVE BEEN DESIGNED BY THE GREATEST OF DESIGNERS."

74

"I HAVE BEEN FASHIONED BY THE GREATEST OF FASHIONERS."

75

"THE MERE FACT THAT
I EXIST PROVIDES ENOUGH
PROOF SIGNIFICANCE
& MEANING TO BE
ALL I NEED TO BE."

76

"I WILL ALWAYS SEEK TO REFINE & FURTHER CORRECT MY PERSPECTIVE."

77

"I DO NOT IDENTIFY WITH POVERTY-CONSCIOUSNESS."

78

"I ONLY IDENTIFY WITH ABUNDANCE-CONSCIOUSNESS."

79

"THE ONLY LACK THAT THERE CAN BE IS THE LACK OF ABILITY TO PERCEIVE OPPORTUNITY."

80

"I HAVE MADE MY MIND UP TO ALWAYS BECOME A GREATER, SUPERIOR VERSION OF MYSELF."

81

"I HAVE MADE MY MIND UP TO SERVE TO THE HIGHEST DEGREE."

82

"I AM CLEAR ON THE DIFFERENCE BETWEEN REWARD & PLEASURE."

(PLEASURE IS NOT ALWAYS REWARD)

83

"ALL THE BEST ANSWERS WILL COME TO ME."

84

"I AM PATIENT
& I AM DETERMINED."

85

"I WILL NOT BE AN AGENT IN MY OWN SELF-DESTRUCTION."

86

"I CREATE POSITIVE, CONSTRUCTIVE, PROSPEROUS HABITS & REINFORCE THEM WITH DAILY PRACTICE."

87

"I THINK OF

REASONS WHY <u>I CAN</u>.

I DO NOT THINK

OF REASONS

WHY I ~~CANNOT~~."

88

"I WILL CONTINUOUSLY IMPROVE THE INTEGRITY OF MY CHARACTER."

89

"I DO & WILL CONTINUE TRUST MY INTUITION."

90

"I AM GUIDED BY DIVINE INSTINCT."

91

"AT THE HIGHEST LEVEL OF IDENTIFICATION ALL IS LIGHT"

92

"ALL OF WHICH I AM PERCEIVING THROUGH MY ORGANIC-EYES IS IN FACT LIGHT."

93

"ALTHOUGH I SEE MANY
DIFFERENT MANIFESTATIONS
OF LIGHT BEFORE ME,
I HOLD STEADILY IN MY
CONSCIOUSNESS THAT ALL
WHICH IS BEING RECEIVED
THROUGH MY ORGANIC EYES
IS BYPRODUCT OF LIGHT,
SIN QUA NONE."

94

"I OPERATE ON THE HIGHEST DEGREES OF IDENTIFICATION, <u>LIGHT & SOUND & MATTER.</u>"

95

"AS ABOVE SO BELOW BUT AS BELOW NOT SO ABOVE."

96

PROSPERTIY IS THE
ONLY PROOF OF MY
INTELIGENCE,
I AM A REFLECTION OF
MY DAILY PROCESS."

97

I DESERVE TO BE
COMPENSATED FOR MY
TIME, ENERGY & SERVICE IF
IT INCREASES THE QUALITY
OF SOMEONE'S LIFE AND/OR
ADDS/CONTRIBUTES TO
THEIR CONVENIENCE OR
WELL-BEING.

98

"THERE IS ALWAYS WORK TO BE DONE."

99

"THE MUTUAL CREATOR OF CREATIONS IS GREATER THAN ALL CREATION"

LISTED IN TABLET FORM

Your World is Yours

1. "I Choose To Only Plant Constructive
   Thoughts Seeds *In The Garden Of My Mind.*"

2. "I Embody Discipline,
   I Embody Principle & Purpose
   Over Caprice & Pleasure."

3. "I Will Read Over These Affirmations
   Twice A Day For 30 Days."

4. "With These Affirmations I Am Making Conscious-
   Constructive Suggestions To
   My Subconscious Mind."

5. "I May Encounter Resistance From Old Ways Of Thinking & I Will Confront Them Directly & Conquer Them With My Ultimate Desire For Corrected Thinking & Thoughts."

6. "My World Is Mine And I Am Its Rightful Master."

7. "My Mind Is Mine & I Shall Feed & Build It In Accordance With Universal Truth."

8. "My Body Is Mine And I Shall Only Feed, Apply And Make Use Of It In A Constructive Way."

9. "*My Soul Is Mine For Eternity* I Am Who I Am & I Will Be Who I Will Be For Eternity."

10. "I Am Blessed & Alive By Means Beyond My Personal Will & Comprehension."

11. "I Have Been Willed Into Existence By The Most Supreme Of ALL Influences & Powers."

12. "The Creator Of All Creation
Has Given Me Everything I Need To Succeed."

13. "It Is Up To Me To Do The
Necessary Work To Manifest The Rest."

14. "*I Devoid Myself Of Entitlement*
& Fully Embrace An EARNING-Mindset."

15. "I Deserve To Exist As Long As I Am Willing
To Earn My Existence & Sustenance."

16. "I Understand That If One Does Not,
Work One May Not Eat, So I Will Earn."

17. "I Operate From Supreme Science
Not Bias, Dogma Or Superstition."

18. "Whatever It Is That I Desire I Will Attract.
So, I Make Sure To Only Desire Constructive Things."

19. "I Love Myself."

20. "I Will Protect Myself _Especially_
From My Destructive Self"

21. "I Respect Myself."

22. "I Am Fully Conscious That I Only Have One Life &
With This One Life I Will Make The Absolute Best Of
It In Honor Of The Fact That I Have Been Willed Into
Existence Independent Of My Own Actions By The
Most Supreme Power In All Of Existence."

23. "I Resonate & Vibrate In Supreme Gratitude Toward
The Highest Of Powers & All Of Existence."

24. "I Will Act In Accordance With My Higher Will."

25. "I Will End All Negotiations With My Lesser Self."

26. "I Do Not Seek A Positive Vibration
As I Am A Positive Vibration."

27. "I Am Eternally Inextricably Linked
To All That Is & All That Will Ever Be."

YOUR WORLD IS YOURS | YWY

28. "I Trust Myself"

29. "I Identify As An Independent INDIVIDUATION & Expression Of All Within ALL & Yet Still Simultaneously Recognize I Am Inextricable To The ALL, Therefore, I Am ALL"

30. "The Greatest Sin Is Perceived Separateness."

31. "The Bigger Picture & Greater Good Are More Important Than My Personal Persona."

32. "I Accept That My Results Are Absolutely Contingent Upon The Quality Of My Actions, I.E., The Quality Of My Conduct."

33. "The Objective Universe Conspires In My Favor As Long As I Am In Accordance With Its Favors, That Is To Say In Favor Of Increased Power & Harmony For All."

113

34. "The Natural Law Of The Universe Is Abundance. Poverty Is ILLNESS."

35. "I Cannot Live Or Be Any Other Way After Affirming These Irrefutable Facts."

36. "I Possess Unlimited Mental Strength."

37. "I Possess Unlimited Spiritual Strength."

38. "I Possess An UNBREAKABLE WILL."

39. "I Change My Thoughts; Therefore, I Change My Life."

40. "I Know Where I Am Going."

41. "The Path Will Illuminate As I Walk It, This Is Because I Am The Light."

42. "I Am Unlimited In Potential."

43. "I Actively Seek To Identify & Detect Any Self-Imposed Limits & In Order To Replace Them With The Unbridled Belief In My Own Abilities."

44. "The Best Things In Life Are Always Attracted To Me."

45. "I Will Feed Myself COURAGE IN THE FACE OF Any Doubt Or Fears."

46. "I PROTECT & INNOCULATE My Mind From All External Impressions NAMLEY Doubt, Fear & Worry."

47. "I Will Always Achieve *Exactly* That Which DESIRE."

48. "I Will Create The Greatest Degree Of Physical, Spiritual, Mental, Emotional, & Existential Satisfaction For Myself."

49. "I Have Faith In The Unseen Forces Which Govern All Of Existence, As Well As My Own Personal Subconscious To See To It That I Achieve Exactly That Which My Heart Desires."

50. "I Am Already Extremely Talented, I Must Masterfully Develop My Talents."

51. "I Am Extremely Skilled I Must Masterfully Develop My Skills."

52. "I Value My Mind, Body & Spirit."

53. "I Do Not Take My Mind, Body & Spirit For Granted; They Are Temporary Gifts From The Divine Which I Did Not Earn & Which Can & Will Be Taken Away."

54. "In This Moment I HAVE EVOLVED & WILL SUSTAIN MY Desire To Evolve For Eternity."

55. "I Become What I Think About Therefore
I Only Think Of Constructive Things."

56. "Houses Do Not Build Themselves Therefore I Must
Remain Constructively Dutiful Toward Myself,
My Life & My Vision."

57. "I Am Dedicated To Personal Excellence
& Personal Development."

58. "I Have A Set Target Before Me."

59. I Hold Crystal-Clear-Visions
Of All That I Would Like To Achieve, Yes, I Do.

60. "I Am Intelligent."

61. "I Possess Great Intellect."

62. "I Am Extremely Knowledgeable In &
On All Subjects Of Earth As Well As The
Whole Boundless Universe."

117

63. "I Am Responsible For My Own Emotions."

64. "I Am Not Personally Responsible For The
Mis-Managed Emotions Of Others."

65. "I Know That My Intent Is Pure."

66. "I Know That I Am Innocent,
Because I Mean No Harm."

67. "There Is No Ill Will In
The Constitution Of My Soul."

68. "I Live To Serve The MOST HIGH
& Never Anything Which Is Even
One Iota Lesser In Degree."

69. "I Will Enlighten All Those
Who Come Across My Path."

70. "Financial Independence Belongs To Me."

71. "I Get Everything That I Ever Want In Life."

72. "I Am One Of The Creator Of Creations Most Favored Creations."

73. "I Have Been Designed By The Greatest Of Designers."

74. "I Have Been Fashioned By The Greatest Of Fashioners."

75. "The Mere Fact That I Exist Provides Enough Proof, Significance & Meaning To Be All I Need To Be."

76. "I Will Always Seek To Refine & Further Correct My Perspective."

77. 'I Do Not Identify With Poverty-Consciousness."

78. "I Only Identify With
Abundance-Consciousness."

79. "The Only Lack That There Can
Be Is The Lack Of Ability To Perceive Opportunity."

80. "I Have Made My Mind Up
To Always Become A Greater,
Superior Version Of Myself."

81. "I Have Made My Mind Up To Serve
To The Highest Degree."

82. "I Am Clear On The Difference
Between Reward & Pleasure."

(Pleasure Is Not Always Reward)

83. "All The Best Answers Will Come To Me."

84. "I Am Patient & I Am Determined."

85. "I Will Not Be An Agent
In My Own Self-Destruction."

86. "I Create Positive, Constructive, Prosperous
Habits & Reinforce Them With Daily Practice."

87. "I Think Of Reasons Why I CAN.
I Do Not Think Of Reasons Why I ~~Cannot~~."

88. "I Will Continually Improve The
Integrity Of My Character."

89. "I Do & Will CONTINUE Trust My Intuition."

90. "I Am Guided By Divine Instinct."

91. "At The Highest Level Of
Identification All Is Light"

92. "All Of Which I Am Perceiving Through
My Organic Eyes Is In Fact, Light."

93. "Although I See Many Different Manifestations Of Light BEFORE Me, I Hold Steadily In My Consciousness That All Being Received Through My Organic Eyes Is A Byproduct Of Light, *Sin Qua None*."

94. "I Operate On The Highest Degrees Of Identification, *Light, Sound & Matter*."

95. "*As Above So Below* But *As Below Not So Above*."

96. Prosperity Is The Only Proof Of My Intelligence, I Am A Reflection Of My Daily Process."

97. "I Deserve To Be Compensated For My Time, Energy & Service If It Increases The Quality Of Someone's Life And/Or Adds/Contributes To Their Convenience Or Well-Being."

98. "There Is ALWAYS Work To Be DONE."

99. "The Mutual Creator Of Creations
   Is Greater Than All Creation."

Made in the USA
Middletown, DE
26 October 2023

41226350R00070